iPhone se 2020

KING N.O

Table of Contents

INTRODUCTION

The first-generation iPhone SE, also known as the iPhone SE 1, is the 9th generation. The idea behind this design was to produce a portable, efficient and an affordable iPhone. For this reason, the advertising slogan is "A big step for the little ones". With the 4-inch screen, users found it easier to navigate the multipurpose touch screen by holding it with one hand. It has almost the same exterior design as its predecessor, the iPhone 5S, but has higher internal hardware, battery capacity and an improved rear camera (12 megapixels), hence the acronym "SE", which means

Special Edition. However, this iPhone was withdrawn on

September 12, 2018 for reasons better known than Apple.

Apple has introduced the iPhone SE 2020, which has been marketed as an affordable smartphone in the phone market to meet the average income, users who love small phones, as well as the successive requirements of the first generation iPhone SE. They did it quite well as this new iPhone is a hybrid of the iPhone 8 and iPhone 11.

It shares the physical dimensions, size, and lens of an iPhone 8 camera, while sharing some of the internal material of the iPhone 11.

DESIGN AND COLOR

The iPhone SE 2020 has a 4.7-inch (diagonal) screen (about thirty percent larger than the first-generation model) with a thick frame above and below the iPhone. The top panel has a stop for speakers, front camera, and sensors, while the bottom panel has a central Home button. The iPhone SE features an aluminum frame, a rear camera on the front and rear, a microphone, and an LED flash. The device has a power button on the right side, a mute button and a volume button on the left, while the speaker holes and the Lightning cable port are located at the bottom. The iPhone SE 2020 is 67.3 mm wide, 138.4 mm high, 7.33 mm thick and weighs 5.22 ounces, so it has the

same physical size as the iPhone 8. This means that the phone cases designed for iPhone 8 can easily fit in iPhone SE 2020.

The iPhone SE 2020 is available in three simple colors: black, white, and red.

Apple says it uses a seven-layer color process to achieve a certain hue, so the aluminum strip matches the color. Available in 64 GB, 128 GB, and 256 GB for users.

A13 BIONIC CHIP SYSTEM

The iPhone SE has the Apple A13 Bionic system on the chip. This is the fastest chip ever designed for a smartphone and therefore provides unmatched performance for any task. This means first-class photography experience, enhanced augmented reality, and great gaming experience. The A13 Bionic chip also provides excellent battery life and power. The iPhone SE also features a third-generation nerve motor and a built-in M13 motion co-processor. With all this, the iPhone SE is one of the most efficient smartphones available in the phone market.

CAMERA

IPhone SE, f / 1.8 aperture, quadruple LED True Tone flash and 4K video (at 24, 30 or 60 fps), 1080p HD video (at 30 or 60 fps) or 720p HD video (at 30 fps). It also offers a 7MP front camera with f / 2.2 aperture and autofocus that can capture 1080p HD video at 30fps. With the A13 Bionic's video signal processor and Neural Engine, the iPhone SE has become the best iPhone of a camera, as it benefits more from computer photography. Using machine learning and monocentric depth estimation, the

front and rear cameras of the iPhone SE support Portrait and Portrait lighting function that captures stunning portraits as well as next-generation Smart HDR images with more natural details. Videos are now more exciting, with better cinematic stabilization and stereo audio recording on both the front and rear cameras. The rear camera supports special videos with extended dynamic range up to 30 fps, as well as high-quality video capture in 4K resolution up to 60 fps. What's even more interesting is that users can now record videos without leaving the photo mode, taking advantage of the QuickTake video on the front and rear camera.

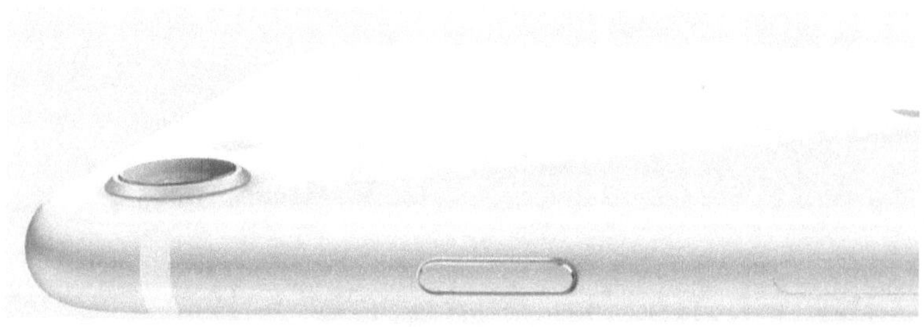

00:00:08

DISPLAY

The iPhone SE features Dolby Vision, which evenly adjusts white-to-ambient balance for a better natural viewing experience, and a wide range of Retina HD displays that support HDR and True Tone playback. The LCD screen has a resolution of 1334 × 750 pixels and a density of 326PPI pixels. iPhone SE uses liver touch for quick actions, such as message preview, live photo animation and application rearrangement.

TOUCH ID

The iPhone SE has a home button
with a Touch ID fingerprint sensor
covered with a steel ring that
detects a user's fingerprint. Touch

ID is used to unlock iPhone, confirm purchases in the App Store, confirm Apple Pay transactions, open password-protected applications, and fill in passwords with the iCloud Keychain. The Touch ID sensor is protected by a durable sapphire crystal.

BATTERY

The iPhone SE uses a 1,821 mAh battery, which supports fast charging. This means it can be charged with a 50% battery life in just 30 minutes and activated using a USB-C power adapter of at least 18 watts and a USB-C Lightning cable. The iPhone SE also supports wireless charging, as it has a glass body with a built-in wireless charging coil that supports Qi-based wireless charging. The battery lasts up to 8 hours of live video playback, up to 13 hours of video playback and up to 40 hours of audio playback.

DOUBLE SIM FEATURE

The iPhone SE supports Dual-Sim functionality, as it allows the use of two phone numbers simultaneously using a physical Nano-SIM and eSIM.

Wireless and BLUETOOTH

iPhone SE supports 2 × 2 MIMO with Wi-Fi 6, which is the latest Wi-Fi protocol and allows up to 38% faster download than other Wi-Fi protocols such as Wi-Fi 5.

It also supports Bluetooth 5.0, which offers faster, wider transmission capacity and greater range.

SOFTWARE

The iPhone SE shipped with iOS 13.4 that supports Apple Pay and Apple Card, and then a software update (iOS 13.4.1) was available the day before the device was released. However, on June 1, Apple released a new iOS 13.5.1 update that can be downloaded for the iPhone SE.

OTHER CHARACTERISTICS

The iPhone SE has an IP67 rating (resistance to dust and water at a maximum depth of 1 meter of water

for up to 30 minutes) according to the standard of the

International Electrotechnical Commission (IEC). This device also has various sensors such as barometer, triaxial gyroscope, accelerometer, proximity sensor and ambient light sensor. Accessibility is not overlooked, as Apple again provides built-in support for hearing aids, touch assist, Siri and dictation, zoom, VoiceOver and many more for people with disabilities. For location services, the iPhone also has a built-in GPS / GNSS, digital compass and iBeacon micro location.

HOW TO INSTALL

Now that you have purchased this new smartphone, setting it up can only be a problem, especially if it is new to the iPhone. As a user, you need to know your options during installation. Among these options.

Set up as a new iPhone - This applies to people who have never used an iPhone or any of Apple's online services.

Restore from previous iPhone - This applies to people who have a previous iOS device and have moved to a new device and want everything they have on the old device to be intact on the new device.

• Transferring data from a phone outside of iOS - This applies to people who switch from a different mobile platform to an iPhone.

Once you understand your options, you are just one step closer to installing your new device. Please note! Before you begin the installation process, you should pay attention to the following:

• A mobile network must be available. For example, the device must be on a Verizon 3G or LTE wireless domain.

• If you are installing in the absence of a mobile network, an active Wi-Fi network must be available.

• Make sure the device is charged. If the battery is empty, use an AC transformer to charge for about 15 minutes.

INSTALLATION AS A NEW IPHONE

• Turn on your new device - Press and hold the side button or power button until the Apple logo appears.

• You will immediately see

"Hello" in different languages. Press the Home button to open the installation and continue.

• Select the language you prefer.

• Select your country or region - This affects the way information is displayed, including the time, date and more, on your device.

• Touch setting manually.

• Select a Wi-Fi network or mobile network depending on what is available.

Apple data and privacy information will be displayed in the next row. After reading, click Continue.

• Touch ID Setup - Click "Set Touch

ID Later" or Continue, and follow the instructions as you are prompted to repeatedly place your thumb or finger on the Enter button. If you are prompted to change your handle, press Continue and place your thumb or finger repeatedly on the Home button, as described, and then click Continue.

• Create Password - Enter a six-digit password or tap "Password Options" if you want a four-digit password or a private password. This is Touch ID, Apple pay, some app purchases, etc. Allows the use of certain features such as.

• Re-enter the given password and click next.

• Application and data - Setup options for how applications and data are transferred to this new device are displayed on the screen.

• Click "Transfer applications and data" to set it as a new device.

• Enter your Apple ID and password. If you don't have an account, you can create a new one. Don't have an Apple ID? and follow the message. Click Next.

• Read and click Accept Apple Terms and Conditions.

• Select Enable location services.

• Apple Pay - Click Continue to set up Apple Pay or click Definition later in the Wallet.

• Click Continue to set the iCloud Keychain or Set Later in Settings.

• Press Continue and "Hey, Siri" or Set later in Settings to Set Siri.

• Continue to set the screen time or set the settings.

• From the App Analytics screen, click Sharing with Application Developers or Sharing (Clicking "Sharing" saves battery life).

• Display - Choose between light or dark screen for your iPhone. Press repeatedly after selecting.

• Screen zoom - Select how you want your screen to be viewed. Typical or deleted. Press repeatedly after selecting.

• You will see the message "Welcome to iPhone".

• Click "Get Started" to start using the iPhone.

RESTORE FROM PREVIOUS IPHONE

This is another way to set up your new device. This procedure

(Quick Start) is possible if your old iPhone and your new iPhone are running iOS 11, 12.4, 13 or later(Note that the iPhone SE 2020 comes with iOS 13.4, so it is compatible with this process). Allows you to quickly transfer information from your old device to new devices wirelessly. Phones must be charged or connected to a power source because the process takes up both the phone and any form of power supply. Interruption can affect data transfer. It's also important to have a backup (iCloud or iTunes) for your data, especially if you're working on older iOS devices (11, 12.4) on your old device before starting this quick boot process to ensure that data is fully transferred to your new device. If your old device is running iOS 13 and then you don't need to back up anything you want.

USE QUICK START

• Turn on your new device - Press and hold the side button or power button until the Apple logo appears.

• You will immediately see "Hello" in different languages. Press the Home button to open it and continue to select the language you prefer.

• Place your new device next to your old device using iOS 11 or later. Immediately, the Quick Launch screen appears on your old device and offers options

Use Apple ID to set up your new device

• Make sure you have the Apple ID you want to use and then click Continue. If you do not see the option to continue on your old device, Make sure Bluetooth is switched on

• An animation will appear immediately on your new device.

• Hold your old device over the new device, then center the animation in the viewfinder of your old device.

• A message saying "New device" "will appear. If you cannot use the camera on your old device, click Authentic Manually, and then

Follow the steps that appear.

• Enter the password of your old device on your new device.

• Follow the instructions to set up Touch ID on your new device or select Set later.

• Transfer your data - This gives you two options. Transfer data from iPhone (old type) or download data from iCloud click Transfer.

Data transfer on your iPhone is faster, especially if your old device is running iOS 13 and later, except that you prefer to download it from an iCloud existing backup.

• Read and click Accept Apple Terms and Conditions.

• Select Adjust or Continue to keep the settings on your old iPhone.

•   Select

Enable location services.

• Apple Pay - Click Continue to set up Apple Pay or click Definition later in the Wallet.

• Press Continue and "Hey, Siri" or Set later in

Settings to Set Siri.

• Click Share or do not share with application developers from the application analysis screen ("Do not share" option saves battery)

• The data transfer screen immediately shows the progress of the transfer to the old device and the new device.

• Wait until the whole process is complete until the "Complete Transfer" message appears on the old iPhone.

• Wait for your new device to restart and start using the downloaded applications in the background.

Viola! Like magic. All your data, including photos, videos, contacts and application data from your old device, is now on your new iPhone SE 2020 in few minutes.

INTRODUCTION OF DATA FROM NON-iOS PHONE

We have smartphone users outside of iOS around the world who often want to share the iPhone experience. That means they have to buy a new iPhone.

So you want to transfer all your data and files from your old smartphone. Apple has an application in the

Google Playstore that makes it possible and it is very easy. The app is called Move to iOS and must be downloaded to the Android phone you already want to transfer.

This is possible with a direct Wi-Fi connection between the Android device and the iOS device. This link is only available with the Move to iOS app and also

While the app runs on iOS 9 and later. This link only transfers photos, contacts, calendars and accounts. It does not transfer applications, music or anything else.

Steps

• Turn on your new device - Press and hold the side button or power button until the Apple logo appears.

• You will immediately see "Hello" in different languages. Press the Home button to open the installation and continue.

• Select the language you prefer.

• Select your country or region - This affects the way information is displayed, including the time, date and more, on your device.

• Touch Setting manually.

• Select a Wi-Fi network or mobile network depending on what is available.

Apple data and privacy information will be displayed in the next row. After reading, click Continue.

• Set Touch ID - Touch "Set Touch ID Later" or Continue and follow the instructions when prompted to place your thumb or finger at home.

Press the button repeatedly. If you are prompted to change your handle, press Continue and place your thumb or finger repeatedly on the Home button, as described, and then click Continue.

• Create Password - Enter a six-digit password or tap "Password Options" if you want a four-digit password or a private password.

These allows features like

Touch ID, Apple payment, some application purchases, etc.

• Re-enter the given password and click Next.

• Application and data - Setup options for how applications and data are transferred to this new device are displayed on the screen.

• Select "Move data from Android".

• Launch the iOS Move app on your Android device

• Click Continue on both devices.

• Click Accept, then tap Next on your Android device.

• Enter the 12-digit code displayed on iPhone on your Android device.

• After entering the password, the Android device automatically connects to your iPhone via Wi-Fi.

• Once logged in, you'll see a list of items you want to transfer to your

Android device. Check any or all and keep going.

• When the transfer is complete, tap Continue iPhone setup.

• Enter your Apple ID and password. If you don't have an account, you can create a new one. Don't have an Apple ID? and follow the message. Click Next.

• Read and click Accept Apple Terms and Conditions.

•   Select

Enable location services.

• Apple Pay - Click Continue to set up Apple Pay or click Definition later in the Wallet.

• Click Continue to set the iCloud Keychain or Set Later in Settings.

• Press Continue and "Hey, Siri" or Set later in Settings to Set Siri.

• Continue to set the screen time or set the settings.

• Tap or Share with application developers from the application analysis screen (choosing not to save battery power)

• Display - Choose between light or dark screen for your iPhone. Press repeatedly after selecting.

• Screen zoom - Select how you want your screen to be viewed. Typical or deleted. Press repeatedly after selecting.

• You will see the message "Welcome to iPhone".

• Click "Start" to start using your new device.

• After that, you will be prompted to sign in to accounts transferred from your Android device.

• Do this and you are ready!

How to introduce Sim contacts to your new iPhone SE 2020

Once you have set up your new device and you are ready to enjoy the iPhone experience without problems, now will be the perfect time to insert the SIM card in your device.

It is very easy to install the SIM card at the transfer point of existing contacts on your new device! All you have to do is:

• Remove the SIM disk using a SIM disk removal tool

• Insert the SIM card correctly into the drive. Note that the SIM card must be Nano SIM.

• Insert the disc containing the SIM into the new device.

• Wait to see if your service line has changed to Operator Network.

•   Go   to

Settings when Cellular Network is available

• Tap People.

• Press Import SIM contacts.

• If prompted, select where you want to enter SIM Contacts.

• Wait patiently for the introduction to complete.

- Open People and make sure your contacts are entered correctly.